How to Run a Successful Business while in High School

Jarrin Christopher Lawton

ISBN-13: 9780692319291
ISBN-10: 0692319298

Library of Congress Control Number: 2015903757
Jarrin Christopher Lawton, Miami, FL

TABLE OF CONTENTS

Acknowledgments

- Family and friends: Thank you to my mother, father, sister, family, and friends, who encouraged me to strive for nothing but excellence. I spent many years compiling the most optimal information for this book.
- Christine E. Babiak: To my beautiful girlfriend, Chrissy, I thank you for all of your support and wisdom in helping me achieve this extravagant life accomplishment.
- Nate Montanez: To my best friend, Nate, I thank you for teaching me about the true values of life.
- President Barack Obama: To my president, I thank you for being a hard worker and reminding me to never give up on the American dream.
- Former/current employees: To my employees, I thank you for your countless amount of time, loyalty, and sweat to get the job done.

- Customers: To my customers, I thank you for the feedback, allowing me to make my service the best around town.
- Miami Dade College (Miami, Florida): To the faculty, staff, and administrators, I thank you for accepting me with open arms.
- Texas Christian University (Fort Worth, Texas): I would like to thank Texas Christian University for the opportunity to continue my education.
- Neeley School of Business (Fort Worth, Texas): I would like to thank the Neeley School of Business for awarding me the Texas Youth Entrepreneur of the Year award.
- St. Pius X High School (Houston, Texas): To the students, faculty, staff, administrators, alumni, and community members, I thank you for your support. I spent many days thanking God for allowing me to transfer into a community of love.

INTRODUCTION

In this book, the main topics will teach you how to run a successful business while in high school. The topics range from operating a budget, managing your social life, and how to study. The majority of the things learned in this book are the real, true facts of being successful while managing a full course load. Going into business while young teaches you a lot about life. It also gives you a better understanding about politics, current events, and the different economic problems that face our country. I will be giving examples of real-time entrepreneurial experiences throughout this book. Wondering why you should start your own business in high school? Well, this book will tell you: free advertising among your peers, support from many local businesses, and you are your own boss.

Chapter 1

WHAT IS AN ENTREPRENEUR?

What is an entrepreneur? An entrepreneur is a person who owns and operates a business and takes an abnormal financial risk to be successful. Being an entrepreneur is really simple; you just have to take risks to reap the benefits. The average entrepreneur fails ten times before the first business succeeds. Entrepreneurship is a skill that is well trained through determination, persistence, and hope. I first learned about entrepreneurship from my grandfather, who owns a limousine business. He taught me the principles of customer service, loyalty, and pride. Being an entrepreneur in the twenty-first century isn't the easiest thing to do. You have to constantly strive for excellence. Also, you have to have the mind-set "I will not fail." Entrepreneurs are strong leaders who are willing to take risks and also take control of the different opportunities our society has given to us. Young entrepreneurship is extremely important because, not only does it teach you to become a better leader, it teaches you financial strategies, economic development, marketing skills, selling practices, and producing a valuable product service at a young age. Being an entrepreneur isn't just about making money; it's about changing the community for the better. As a young entrepreneur, many doors will open and close at the same time. You have to gain the trust of other people at a young age.

Chapter 2

BECOMING A BUSINESS-MINDED TEENAGER

This chapter is one of the most important in this book. Because it teaches you key tools to become a business-minded teenager. One of the first steps of becoming a business-minded teenager is wanting to make money. There's only one thing that businesses set out as their mission, and that's to make a profit. Profit is the amount of money a business makes after all of the expenses are complete. So if you're asking, "How do you make a profit?" I have three steps that will help you gain and achieve the highest profit as a young entrepreneur. The first is research.

Research goes beyond reading a book or listening to news. When you're researching information for your business, you have to dig deep into the surface. Most entrepreneurs think this can be done by going to your local library or reading things online about the topic you are pursuing. Using that method of research is good, but it's not the best. The best type of research I have found is to seek out experience, such as asking local business owners and other entrepreneurs about the topics you're interested in. There's key information that business owners will give you that books and texts will not share. The next step of making a profit is marketing.

Marketing is when you have to promote the service or products you are trying to sell to your general customer base. Marketing yourself as a young entrepreneur with a new business is a difficult thing to do. There are new tools in the twenty-first century that allow you to market yourself and your business easier than ever before. Tools, such as the Internet, help you market easily because you are reaching out to your target audience at a rapid speed rate. It also allows you to channel out the clientele you are seeking so that you won't waste time and resources. Last but not least, we have selling.

Selling is a skill that one masters to retain the business of a customer. When a customer is purchasing a product or your services, they are buying into you. As an entrepreneur, you are the living aspect and creator of your product or service. You have to act like an adult and be informative about your trade. Once you master the art of selling, it's up to you to keep grinding. Being a business-minded teenager isn't always about making money. As a young entrepreneur, you will see that business is great, but the community you operate in deserves the true reward.

The reward of love is an attitude you have to train yourself to understand. Even though money is why a business operates, it's the community you serve or sell to that deserves the thanks. In becoming a young successful entrepreneur, you have to understand how to give back. It can be as simple as spending twenty dollars to purchase pizza and soda for a local school's field trip or sponsoring a child to play T-ball. As a business owner, you are expected to have strong ethics. The best way to keep good in your community is to give back and allow more ideas and dreams to grow and become a success like yourself.

Chapter 3

LISTEN. OBSERVE. LABOR.

Listen. Observe. Labor. These words make up the LOL topic that I will be discussing. First we have listen. Listening has to be one of the most difficult aspects of becoming a young and successful entrepreneur because listening is the skill that you have to acquire to understand the key principles of other people's advice and knowledge. Most young people listen and retain information but don't grasp the key elements. It can be as simple as listening to your teachers speak about an important topic in class or when customers are giving you feedback regarding your product or services. Training your mind to hear the importance of all aspects makes you a better listener. For example, I listened to established small-business owners about how to properly start a small business before starting up shop. Listening to your advisors brings you key insight, which isn't taught in a textbook or on Google. This brings me to the next topic, which is observe.

Observation is a silent tool that successful entrepreneurs and students use to master their hidden skills when implementing success. When you observe something of importance, make detailed notes. Outline the importance of each subject's main points. When you master the skill of observation, you can silently go to work. Sometimes it's better to observe and learn what is being done before making your entrance into the marketplace. For example, I started with a small observation of an eighteen-wheeler super truck pressure washer cleaning a racetrack before I started business operations. It was a time of listening and observation, which brings me to the last topic labor. Labor is the easiest but most complex of all the LOL topics.

Labor is simply described as putting the work in for maximum results. This is better referred to as "grinding." It doesn't matter if it's studying two hundred flash cards for a test or cutting twenty yards a week. Labor has to be done with care and love. Why? When you put care and love into your labor, you are giving yourself to the cause. And that cause is being successful—to become the best student you can be by studying for four hours or being the best landscaper by devoting time, effort, and sweat to make a yard look like the yard of the month. For example, I would wake up at six o'clock in the morning during the summer to get my cleaning equipment and supplies ready for potential customers. Some days there would be no customers calling, but I was still ready to go work.

Chapter 4

HOW TO USE SOCIAL MEDIA

Social media is used to interact with existing and potential customers on a massive scale. Social media is just as important as making a profit. Using social media the proper way can mean everything to a new start-up business or a young entrepreneur's success. There are many different forms of social media, but the three main types are social networking, content communities, and microblogs. First we have social networking. Social networking is a social structure that allows businesses to directly communicate to their customers, allowing you to communicate to the masses. It allows for easier growth and development.

Social networking is also a tool that can be used for tracking customers' histories and living patterns. The largest social network firm, Facebook, allows businesses to post upcoming events and invite people to their groups. Secondly, there are the content communities. Content communities are online communities where users can share different information with others. These communities are good for companies because you can post information about your business and receive information about others. These communities, such as YouTube, are good for advertising and marketing, as well as social networking. The last type of social media I am discussing is microblogging. Microblogging is a form of social media in which the content of the blog is much smaller than average blogging. Users and businesses can communicate with short messages—about anything, really. Microblogs, such as Twitter, are being used every day to help businesses communicate and spread the word much easier.

One of the most advanced forms of social media now is picture sharing. For example, as a business, you can send images of new products and services directly to your existing or potential customers' smartphones via Instagram. As technology changes and advances, we, as entrepreneurs, must change and adapt ASAP.

Chapter 5

HOW TO STUDY

Studying is really simple; you just have to do the work. It's actually not that easy. Studying is reviewing the information you have previously learned. I have included three things that are conducive to studying: review, recite, and reflect. A review is an evaluation of a specific topic. This goes beyond reviewing for an exam; it could be reviewing paperwork before a contract is finalized. The review phase is crucial for the recite phase. The reciting phase is when one repeats information out loud. This helps build great memory skills for class and for business. Last of the studying skills is reflecting. Reflecting is a skill that is difficult for most adults to learn. Reflection is when one looks back into the past and remembers what has been done or taught to you. Using any form of studying is always a huge help.

I had a weak study ethic, but I always asked for help. Studying for anything gives you a huge advantage. Whether it's a final exam or tests to get certified in a trade, always remember the three Rs: review, recite, and reflect.

Chapter 6

MANAGING YOUR SOCIAL LIFE

Social life is an entrepreneur's best and worst feature at the same time. Why? As an entrepreneur, your number-one commitment is to make your investment back and reap the benefits of having your own business. By being a young entrepreneur in high school, things may seem a little weird. I thought high school was an amazing learning tool to implement things you learn in school into your day-to-day life. You won't have the same free time as your peers. It's difficult not having a social life at times, because you are growing up with your peers, and you want to have fun. I'll be the first to tell you that, when you put your head down and grind, the fame of high school and life will come to you eventually. Here are a few steps I have learned through trial and error that can help you.

Take advantage of all the free time you have while at school to study and complete your homework. Also, if you commute to school via bus or car, start doing your work on the road. Most teenagers give the same excuses: "I don't have time to do that," or, "I'm tired." Making the most of study halls at school and the commute will free up some time for business.

Teenagers don't understand that, as a young adult, you start to receive the privileges and consequences of an adult. For example, while your peers are having fun going to the movies or out to eat on Friday and Saturday nights, you are doing work for the business. We, as entrepreneurs, have to believe the mind-set that one day all of our hard work will pay off. Hard work and persistence will make your life as an entrepreneur a lot easier. Beginning at a young age and practicing your networking and socializing skills will allow you to be a jack-of-all-trades.

Chapter 7

SURROUND YOURSELF WITH A

POSITIVE ENVIRONMENT

In this day and age, you are just as good as the company you keep. Surround yourself with positive people who are going to push you toward greatness, and you'll be a positive person. Only keep positive attributes around, because (one) it reflects on you as a person and (second) as a business owner. I have lived through high school, and there is a lot of peer pressure to do things like drinking as a minor or smoking. You, as an entrepreneur, have to want to be great.

Oprah Winfrey said, "I always believed I would be great." I realize that, as an entrepreneur, you may not know what product to sell or what service to offer. You have to constantly believe in yourself and have positive people in your inner circle. As humans, we see people who already are or becoming successful, and we can't see why they are successful.

Being an entrepreneur is not always about the people you surround yourself with to create a positive atmosphere but also about giving positive vibes to others. Bob Marley said it best: "The greatness of a man is not in how much wealth he acquires but in his integrity and his ability to affect those around him positively."

Money isn't the only principle to validate a person's credibility. I will tell you the truth; money counts for 100 percent of a business's financial credit, but a person's honesty and morals go longer than money. When you strive for excellence to achieve greatness and not to make the most money, you are rewarded with the satisfaction of doing something great. Remember what I JUST SAID! Don't become focused on just making money and profit.

Chapter 8

DO WHAT YOU LIKE!

Being your own boss is the greatest achievement of mankind from the entrepreneur's perspective. In this chapter, I will tell you the truth that some adults won't tell you. I know some of you reading this don't have products for sale or business services you are offering just yet, and that's perfectly fine. You have to make sure you know what you want to do first, because you have to put your heart and soul into your labor. Selecting what is best for you will take some time.

I'm going to address the main topic, which is highlighted in the title of this book, and that is school. Doing what you like doesn't mean just doing business without continuing your education. You will have freedom once you graduate high school, and it's up to you—and only you—to continue pursuing education.

This is coming from a young, successful entrepreneur who had everything in high school. I was on top of the charts in the state of Texas. In 2010, I was named the TCU Texas Youth Entrepreneur of the Year.

This is an award given to the best candidate among twenty-five young entrepreneur finalists who are all amazing business-minded entrepreneurs in their respected fields. I tell you this because you can have positive things going on in business, and that's great, but at the end of the day, an education means everything to society. With that being said, college students are graduating with bachelor's degrees and not getting hired. This is a sign of the times evolving in America and the rest of the world. What do I mean by "sign of the times?" About thirty years ago, graduating with a bachelor's degree was all you needed. Now college students have to stay in college longer and go deeper into debt to gain their master's degree just to get hired. Are you wondering what to do? The best thing for you to do is follow your dreams and strive for nothing but excellence in whatever endeavors your path leads you to.

Chapter 9

FOCUS

Staying focused can be extremely tough while in high school. Your mind is on alert for several things: studying, extracurricular activities, and your business goals. I have learned that the human brain is just like a sponge. It soaks up small pieces of knowledge and allows us to channel the information learned, using it for the better of humanity. Here are a few tools to stay focused. Allow yourself to do the creative things first. Our brains like doing the fun things first, leading up to the difficult tasks. Secondly, use your time wisely. Too often time is wasted because we aren't doing the proper things for success or we're just being lazy. This brings me to the third focusing method.

Train your mind like a muscle. Start small with tasks and slowly grow into something larger, allows your mind to adapt. It's just like getting a six-pack; you have to constantly work and grind to get results.

You aren't going to get focused overnight. It takes hard work to master the art of focusing.

Chapter 10

MAKING IT OFFICIAL

Become a proud business owner by making your small-business dream a reality. It may seem difficult while in high school, but it's very simple. Instead of using your allowance or birthday money on a video-game system, invest that money into a DBA (Doing Business As) license. Do the research at your local county clerk's office online, or call to find the requirements for your county. After you know what you need, go to your county clerk's office, and tell them you want to file a business name. File the paperwork, and then you are a registered business. You can then perform business under the name you filed. This is an awesome validation for a young business owner in high school.

Next, depending on what your product or service is, you may be required by state or federal law to be an insured business. Word of advice: if you aren't required to be insured, get insurance anyway. Most consumers and other businesses won't work with you if you aren't insured. Being under the age of eighteen, you may have difficulty with this, but ask your guardian for help with the process.

Next is the fun part of exposing your business to your customer base. Using social media and word of mouth, you can start marketing for free! I advise you to get a free website or a cheap monthly hosting site so that you can have a place where your clients can validate you. There are other forms of validation, such as the BBB (Better Business Bureau), and networks where experienced businesses have organizations validating them to customers. This is the direction you should pursue after getting started.

April is called the most hectic time of the year. Do you have any idea what it is? If you guessed tax season, you guessed correctly. As a business, you are required to pay taxes. Some of the advantages businesses have are tax deductions. Tax deductions are the items business can write off for a tax credit. You have to pay a certain percentage to the federal and state governments for making money. It's how the government keeps afloat. My advice is to find a local CPA (certified personal accountant) to help you organize your finances.

Making things official takes time and persistence so that your operation will be a well-oiled machine.

Chapter 11

RUNNING THE BUSINESS
DURING SCHOOL

Managing a business during school hours isn't the easiest thing to do. I'm going to give you examples of how to keep operations flowing smoothly while you're in school. I had ten employees cleaning apartment complexes while I was a senior in high school. The key is finding employees you can trust. I used my free time at school to respond to e-mails and communicate with my customers.

Since you are the business owner, remember that you are liable for all work being done while you aren't on-site. I taught my employees the same principles I use while cleaning. You're never too young to take action, whether it's for school or business. In fact, taking action, in general, is the best form of being proactive, be it trying to make up homework you missed in class or to correct a mistake you had on the job site.

Chapter 12

GET A MENTOR

My mentor, news anchor Iain Page.

Every young business owner needs some form of advice. I learned at an early age that, if you have questions about something, you shouldn't be afraid to ask. Asking questions is the best way to gain information, because experience and wise advice are always better than finding out about a subject the hard way. I had several mentors while I was in high school. I chose the universal method, meaning every adult who spoke to me, I took certain things they said and built a damn good foundation. Below are examples of the mentors in my life.

- Parents: taught me to be me and only me
- Grandparents: were there for the wise advice
- Aunts and Uncles: helped me with whatever was needed
- Cousins: were my support team and my number-one fans
- Friends: had my back, no matter what happened
- Teachers: taught me key leadership tools
- Church life: taught me how to stay strong when things weren't always so good
- Business owners: told me how to do things the right way once
- Police officers: guided me through what was right for society
- Government officials: taught me nothing! (They showed me that nothing will work if you can't get along with each other.)

- Everyday citizens: taught and continue to teach me that we are all human beings and deserve for our voices to be heard

Getting a mentor to assist you with your entrepreneur questions and about life is the best form of help. You have to research the person before asking them to be your mentor. The objective is to gain information about different topics and get the advice needed for proper development. Mentors act as advisors for our daily lives. They help us focus and keep us on track based on their previous experiences in life.

Chapter 13

SAVE YOUR MONEY

Now it's time to address one of the hardest _and_ easiest things to do. Saving your money may seem frustrating, because you worked for your money and you want to spend your earnings. The five ways I was taught to save money were to learn self-control, take control of my financial future, know where my money goes, start an emergency fund, and start saving for retirement now. The first money-saving method is learning self-control. Having self-control when it comes to saving money is a habit that you have to be taught or learn the hard way. For example, when you graduate high school, there will be many options for you to receive money you don't have.

The easiest forms of free money are credit cards. Credit-card companies will reel you in with no interest and give you a small balance to spend, without telling you the harm it does to your credit. Credit is the single most important aspect of a business, other than profit. Once you mess it up, it's ten times harder to fix it. Having self-control to say, "No, I don't need that," and continue to grind until you can pay cash for something is the best way to go. Taking control of your financial future at a young age is the key for a fruitful lifestyle in your later years. Do your research on the different types of financial intuitions, and stay informed about the economy.

Many youngsters don't understand the financial systems of life during or after college. Get yourself a financial advisor, and plan out your future. This brings me to my next method, and that is to know where your money goes. As a young adult, you may have some understanding about financial systems. You need to know all the aspects of the financial system and have knowledge of where all of your money is a must. Creating a monthly budget will allow you to see where your money is going in and out. This method allows you to cross-reference the money that was allocated to spend with the actual money spent. The next method of saving is to start an emergency fund. Having emergency money of your own is always crucial for a rainy day. Emergency funds can be money you saved from every paycheck for a down payment on a car or house or for a vacation you've been planning for sometime.

Lastly is to start saving for retirement now. It may seem funny talking about retirement while you're still in high school, but this is a huge part in having a happy stable life in the long run. Think about creating an IRA (individual retirement account). I opened up an IRA account at Edward Jones financial advisors when I was sixteen. You will need your guardian to open this account with you. It's called a custodial account because you are underage. This account allows you to save your money and invest it to gain interest over time. Even if you can just invest fifty dollars a month into the account, that's six hundred dollars in a year toward your financial freedom.

Remember that anybody can save money. It's up to you to use the different ways to funnel your money for the maximum benefits at the end of the road.

Chapter 14

LEARN UNDER FIRE

Learning under fire is when you are learning as you go. You have to deal with the unexpected as it arises. For example, in March 2010, I was served papers at school because I was being accused of not paying a former employee. The process was extremely long and painful, but I took action. I stood my ground as a young business owner and fought until the end. I had testimonies from five of my employees, stating that I did pay this employee in cash, but that was the only record I had of payment. I had to learn the hard way that there are sneaky people up to no good in the world. I eventually settled this matter and paid an undisclosed amount to the plaintiff. I would have gone to court, but it wasn't worth my time and effort for the small amount of money the plaintiff was seeking. At that point, I made the decision to choose battles wisely. I could have gone to court, but I would have been wasting time, money, and resources on something that meant nothing to me.

Chapter 15

FOCUS ON COMPANY CULTURE

Creating a positive company culture is the hidden secret behind your businesses success. Company culture starts with you, the entrepreneur. Your employees observe your positive attitude. And one thing is a happy employee is a happy business. When you have a happy business, you have happy customers. As a young entrepreneur, people look up to you because you have taken the risk already, but doing small things to make your employees happy shows true leadership. I would pay my employees nothing less than ten dollars an hour. This was an incentive because it was extremely high to my employees, but I knew paying my employees a high wage would mean no problems.

By having a positive company culture, you aren't required to do anything else, but you can treat your employees on performance and just doing the right thing. About twenty percent of the week, I would treat my employees to breakfast, lunch, or dinner, just as a thank you. Be it fast-food or a sit-down meal, just showing your appreciation means every-thing. We are all human beings and just want the common courtesy of respect, peace, and love.

Chapter 16

EDUCATE YOUR CUSTOMERS

By now you have likely given some form of speech in high school. Public speaking is a dynamic tool you have to use to communicate among others. A well-known professor of speech and debate at a local university in Houston, Texas, said, "You speak before you speak." What I have grasped is that you have to master your verbal and nonverbal skills. This is the same in speech and business.

In business you have to educate your customers by speaking to them, not at them. When you educate your customers about your services, your gestures and knowledge must be tuned up to the max. It is important to give your customers the proper information the first time so that you won't have to correct yourself. For example, I am in the cleaning industry. For me it is really simple to overlook the small details of a job. For the customer, what it means to do a soft wash on a roof may be confusing. By educating your clients step-by-step, you are allowing the customers to learn and understand the service they have purchased. Secondly, they will feel more comfortable with you because you have educated them and they know what to expect. It's all about the communication you have with your customer.

CONCLUSION

As you can see, I have outlined several key points on how to run a successful business while in high school. The main things to keep in mind from reading this book are remembering what an entrepreneur is, listening to those key mentors in your life, and focusing in school. School is going to be difficult, no matter how smart you are. It's up to you to master the system and want to be successful. Until next time, keep grinding.

Photo Credits

- Front-cover photo: The Neeley Entrepreneurship Center

- Chapter 12 photo: Iain Page

- Back-cover photo: The Neeley Entrepreneurship Center

www.ingramcontent.com/pod-product-compliance
Lightning Source LLC
Chambersburg PA
CBHW071749020426
42331CB00008B/2234